BETHANY BELL

Photography by Ken Cheal

on being single

Ark House Press
PO Box 1722, Port Orchard, WA 98366 USA
PO Box 1321, Mona Vale NSW 1660 Australia
PO Box 318 334, West Harbour, Auckland 0661 New Zealand
arkhousepress.com

© Bethany Bell 2019

Unless otherwise stated, all Scriptures are taken from the New Living Translation (Holy Bible. New Living Translation copyright© 1996, 2004, 2007, 2013 by Tyndale House Foundation. Used by permission of Tyndale House Publishers Inc., Carol Stream, Illinois 60188. All rights reserved.)

Cataloguing in Publication Data:
Title: On Being Single
ISBN: 9780648458562
Subjects: Relationships; Single; Christian Living
Other Authors/Contributors: Bell, Bethany

Design by initiateagency.com

This book is dedicated to
the one who *knows* and *loves* my heart the most.

Whom have I in heaven but you? You're all I want! No one on earth means as much to me as you. Psalm 73:25 TPT

Hi there.

For me, this would be a random book to read, let alone write!
So, why did I write it?

I have penned these words to bring light to a subject that is often treated, let's be honest, *awkwardly*. These writings address misconceptions, present ideas and share experiences centred on my life and observations as a single person. It is my hope that we transition from awkward to real freedom that stems from knowing God and following Him.

These thoughts have shaped my thinking, grown me as a person and changed me over time. I pray they do the same for you, I also hope you enjoy the read!

Bethany

Please note: *some names and identifying details have been changed to protect the privacy of individuals.*

Contents

STRAIGHT TALK

Punch You In The Face!.. 2
A Short Story 5
Singleness Isn't Fair 7
Illogical Logic 10
The Shelf 15

DEALING WITH STUFF

Masquerade Ball 20
Celebrate 24
Driven By The External 29
Expectations 31
A Heroine 34

IN THE REAL WORLD

Some Days 38
Intimacy 44
Fear and Desire 46
Puzzles 50
Expression 52

LIVING THE DREAM

Unknown 59
Thankfully 61
Whimsical Staircase 62
Brick Castles 65
Dream 68

Bye for now 71
Photographer 72
Thank You 73

Punch You In The Face!

I was sitting in church when the guest preacher took to the stage. I had only heard this speaker once before and unlike those around me, who were eating up every word, I sat more as a sceptic. It was this that largely contributed to the feelings that were about to rush through me.

I cannot remember what the speaker's topic was. I did recall, however, a story he told about his years at Bible College, or 'Bridal College' as he jokingly called it. He painted a picture of all the good-looking women he met, leading to one in particular whom he found extremely attractive. My scepticism was rising.

He looked to see if this girl was wearing a wedding ring. No! Bingo! He went on to explain why she may or may not be married. He recounted that considering she was a good-looking young blonde, she would either be married or dating. His investigations found that she was still single and therefore, he began his pursuit of her.

His story was common enough. Cute even! It was the social commentary that went with the story that raised my ire. In the midst of his explanation, he said: *"because we all know that everyone good-looking in the church is married by 22"*. **I nearly hit the roof!**

Let me confess here; I wasn't exactly feeling holy anger! To be truthful, I was overcome with the desire to punch him square in the face! I am a pretty calm customer, but as his carefree commentary hit the crowd, I was incensed. Why?

Because it is categorically untrue!

And statements like these not only have the power to paint marriage as some type of trophy for those at the top of the social hierarchy, but they fuel misconceptions. Misconceptions that hurt everyone.

To those friends who don't make us feel like we're third wheeling; we love you!

A Short Story

A few years ago, I was relaying a story about a boy I liked in my teen years when, in complete shock, my sister blurted out "you liked someone!" I laughed, equally surprised at her response, as the fabricated image of me she held came crashing down.

I am sure we have all liked someone (or many someone's!) over the years. There are those we like and then there are, well, those we *really* like.

There was one such man some years ago. We attended the same church and within time ended up serving in the same ministry. True to form, I prayed that God would take away the feelings if they weren't from Him.

They stayed.

This guy was ideal, AND he had dark hair (always a winner!) I observed this person in a variety of situations and my admiration increased. It was safe to say, I *really* liked this guy!

One night, whilst sitting in bed, I was conversing with God about the person I would like to date. I couldn't quite find the phrase, 'I want to marry someone adventurous'. Instead, it came out as "I want to marry someone who jumps off cliffs and stuff." (*I know, I know, I am so eloquent!*) Unexpectedly, two days later, this man was returning something he had borrowed. During our conversation, he showed me a video from his weekend - jumping off cliffs!

My puzzle pieces were *falling into place*.

I began to think about this guy and the possibility of a relationship more often. Before I knew it, I was thinking about him, about us, *all* the time.

There was nothing to deter me from this guy; his qualities endeared me, his good looks attracted me and with no girls on the scene it seemed so right! Did we have a winner?!

My thoughts about him continued to be more constant, more repetitive, more one track. I had become obsessed and I did not like it.

I am not inclined to have obsessions about anything. I was getting extremely frustrated at myself and the mystery of whether this puzzle was the right puzzle. One day pent up in frustration and *extremely* fed-up, I sat on my bed, vented to God and said, **"you need to tell me"**.

As clear as day, God said: "let it go"!

In that moment, I chose to let it go.

Within a short time, I found out he had a serious girlfriend.

Do I think this will or should happen every time I like someone? Certainly not! God does not work in rules. We live in relationship with Him.

The key to living a contented single life isn't a cookie-cutter method of five steps. It is about our relationship with God, being real, growing in wholeness and building healthy relationships around you.

Our personal lives are a journey, not systematic steps to success.

Singleness Isn't Fair

Have you ever compared your relationship status to another's and been left wanting?
Have you ever felt like you're coming last in a race to the altar?
Perhaps you've seen a relationship as the reward you deserved, but didn't receive, for years of serving God?

Recently an acquaintance of mine got engaged. A colleague relayed their engagement story and on this day, I was in no particular mood to hear the news, or, rejoice. I wish I could say that I was happy for them, but I wasn't feelin' it.

Maybe because I had a lot on my mind. Maybe I just don't really know this person. Maybe it was because I had been contemplating the fact that sometimes there is no rhyme or reason as to why some people get married and others don't. Whatever the reason, my attitude wasn't godly. I repented of this attitude, yet, was still left contemplating the concept of *fairness*.

Truth be known, we want life to be fair. We want our singleness to be based on something; whether we are good looking (according to whose standards, anyway), whether we've been diligent in self-care, whether we've worked hard for a good career, whether we've been obedient to Christ, whether we've remained sexually pure or not, we may even surmise that we don't have the levels of godliness or sacrificial love that is required in marriage; we desperately grasp for *anything* in order to make sense of our singleness.

A relationship is not a prize for our faithfulness any more than singleness is a result of faithlessness; this is a form of works-based theology.

Marriage is not a prize!

Like singleness, marriage is one of the many gifts God gives in the human experience, not a reward or even a guaranteed outcome.

Often it is assumed that singleness is a waiting season for married life. Though singleness can lead to dating and marriage, *we are not in a waiting line.* We are *all,* single and married alike, in this beautiful thing called *life*, where God is continually growing and changing us. We do not graduate into seasons when we are ready, we follow Jesus through all the questions, transitions, lack of readiness, beauty and mess to be made like Him.

I was talking with someone very dear to me the other day. They were offloading their feelings about their season of singleness, concluding that *life isn't fair*. She was looking for that black and white reason that explained why she was single and others were not.

We too often look for these measures to provide reason and clarity, as though our circumstances or marital status are the measures for God's favour. *Preposterous!*

God's character must be the looking glass for our lives and our perspective based on His truth, not circumstances.

Have you ever made an assumption as to why you are still single?

Illogical Logic

Have you ever made an assumption as to why you are still single? Maybe you've given a friend a reason (or several reasons) why you haven't met someone.

'I need to lose weight and then I'll meet someone.'
'Once I become financially stable, then God will bring someone into my life.'
'If I was more intelligent or had attended university; that would have changed things.'
'Perhaps, if I was better socially, and didn't choke up each time he or she spoke to me.'

Sure, these things may hold some truth; it may be healthy for you to become disciplined in fitness, learn budgeting skills, to pursue study or further develop your social skills. Some changes may even open up your dating options! But they are not the reason you are single.

How do I know?

Because both fit and overweight people, Brainiac's and TV addicts, the party animals and the recluses… all types of weird and wonderful people get married. Every single day!

In an attempt to explain to ourselves and others why we are single we think ourselves into illogical reasoning. The small elements of truth cause us to buy into the incorrect mindset. This illogical reasoning is found in a false image, as it denies your value and what you bring, as well as, God's opinion and timing. It gives permission for insecurity and justification to control your heart attitude rather than love and acceptance.

These mindsets are often drawn in comparison to others and centre on the belief that we lack something. Comparison always causes *someone* to come up short, robbing value from either yourself or another person. Quit with comparison, and allow truth to become your mindset. We are *all* "works in progress" don't allow other people, circumstances or even yourself to determine your value. Take your question of value to the source.

Some months ago, I was walking in obedience to what I know God asked me to do. Yet, I couldn't see the productivity I was used to as a youth pastor who had run programs, a personal assistant who had gigantic task lists or as a student who impatiently waited for grades on essays. Each season I had lived so far had a way for me to *measure my value*.

But not this season.

This season didn't have a job description or a boss checking up, or even a task list to which someone held me accountable. It was full of unchartered and unknown paths of conversations and creative pursuits to love and serve people.

When was enough, enough? Was I doing all that God required? Is this what He had in mind? What do people think I do, 'nothing, that's what!' … and even; how will any single guy think "yep, she's the one!" I don't even have a "normal" job, earn an income or have a list of achievements to stand upon.

That's right, I had nothing to stand on.

Sometimes God allows a strong confrontation to get our attention. God will pull the comforts of carpet from underneath us until we remain standing on Him, our firm foundation.

I over-analysed myself into a stalemate position; I thought myself into a frenzy; took on the perceived expectations of others, and allowed these, along with my own standards and questions to ring in my ears. *I couldn't find a way out.*

Then, one day while washing up, as a question seeking affirmation was about to spill from my lips, I felt God whisper *"bring your question of value to me!"* Unsure what that even looked like, I slowly turned my attention to seek God in this question rather than others.

Many of us search for validation, in varied forms and places, but there is only one place in which the question of value can truly be answered.

During a prayer day for our region, a friend mentioned a verse in passing; 'great verse!' I thought. Over the following days, this verse crept slowly into my heart until it made its home there.

> *For the source of your pleasure is not in my performance or the sacrifices I might offer to you. The fountain of your pleasure is found in the sacrifice of my shattered heart before you. You will not despise my tenderness as I humbly bow down at your feet.*
> Psalm 51:16-17 TPT

The source of God's pleasure, where we know our value, is not found in our performance, our measurements, our achievements, appearance or circumstances; where would that leave the poor? Where does that leave those whom societies deem undesirable? What does that say about someone who holds a trade or degree verse someone who does not? No no!

Our value is found in knowing God's pleasure, and God's pleasure is found as we surrender our lives to Him.

> *Stop imitating the ideals and opinions of the culture around you, but be inwardly transformed by the Holy Spirit through a total reformation of how you think. This will empower you to discern God's will as you live a beautiful life, satisfying and perfect in his eyes.*
> *Romans 12:2 TPT*

Your value is not determined by your external circumstances, your performance or other, it is crowned upon you without condition. It is irrevocable, but your perception can attempt to tell you otherwise. Shift your focus onto the Holy Spirit, allow Him to work a total reformation of how you think. *Take your question of value to the source.*

> *And because God is the source and sustainer of everything, everything finds fulfilment in him.*
> *Romans 11:36a TPT*

Following this, if there remain areas that you desire to see a change in, instead of living in a world of 'if only I was…', change it or accept that it's not changing just yet.

How did we ever talk ourselves into some of these illogical assumptions and accept them as truth? They have led to a perceived reduction of value and greatly contribute to our view of singleness, leading us to feel the need to explain to ourselves and others why we are still single.

Perhaps the extent to which we feel the need to explain our singleness corresponds with our revelation around value.

And I pray that He would unveil within you the unlimited riches of His glory and favour until supernatural strength floods your innermost being with His divine might and explosive power.

Then, by constantly using your faith, the life of Christ will be released deep inside you, and the resting place of His love will become the very source and root of your life.

Then you will be empowered to discover what every holy one experiences—the great magnitude of the astonishing love of Christ in all its dimensions. How deeply intimate and far-reaching is His love! How enduring and inclusive it is! Endless love beyond measurement that transcends our understanding—this extravagant love pours into you until you are filled to overflowing with the fullness of God!

Never doubt God's mighty power to work in you and accomplish all this. He will achieve infinitely more than your greatest request, your most unbelievable dream, and exceed your wildest imagination! He will outdo them all, for His miraculous power constantly energizes you.
Ephesians 3:16-20 TPT

The Shelf

I remember being in the college library engaged in conversation with a fellow classmate. We were discussing her recent twentieth birthday and the conversation turned to relationships. She made a statement I will never forget;

> "If I am not married by twenty-two, I will be on the shelf".
> 'What?!'

At 18, marriage was not in the forefront of my mind and the idea of being married did not serve to keep me off *some shelf*.

Somewhere in our lives, we can allow the concept of 'the shelf' to settle and be accepted.

The shelf is a self-assigned place where people resign themselves to singleness forever. The shelf is defined differently for different people. For some it is defined by a certain age, like for my friend; for many, it is a standard of beauty; for others, the shelf is resigned to after experiencing too many broken hearts (one too many). For you, it may be something else, but whatever the reason, many settle for 'the shelf'.

You may not have settled for 'the shelf' yet, however, you see it as an approaching doom that you are attempting to avoid, at all costs. Others, a self-assessment that, 'I am not good enough for a relationship,' has caused some to resign themselves to the looming inevitability of 'the shelf'. For many singles, fear of 'the shelf' has been the driver in making some bad relationship decisions. Others have already accepted their place on 'the shelf', living there as if locked in a jail, without any choice.

I was in my late-teens chatting with friends in the lounge room, at the same time could over-hear friends in the kitchen talking about what age we'd all get married. As you would, I successfully continued conversing while listening to the entertaining conversation coming from the kitchen. One friend remarked, "Oh Bethany, she won't get married till she's older, like 26 or something!"

It went straight for my heart.

I had no plans to get married anytime soon, yet that seed took root and over the years the words spoken became my approaching doom. 'Was I too independent?' 'Was I not good enough?' 'Why was I the one to be married late, *the last man standing*?' Whatever their reasoning, 26 haunted me, if I wasn't married by then I was *old*, as my friend had put it.

My 26th birthday drew nearer and nearer, there was no partner in sight. I had accepted the lies that I wasn't good enough, that I was, *of course,* the last one standing and that age mattered.

I told you this was straight talk, I won't beat around the bush. We all have issues and secrets; some things never spoken, words said over our lives that have never heard the truth, past experiences we feel we can never escape, lies we have accepted, memories that haunt us, hurts we carry, rejection piled in our hearts.

I get it.

Let me tell you the *one moment* this all turned around for me?

I can't! There wasn't one.

Sorting through our "stuff" can be done in a moment, but more often than not, it is a journey. I no longer carry these lies around nor does age haunt me like it once did. I live in freedom knowing whatever words spoken, things experienced, hurts carried, no matter how high my pile of "stuff" it's never too much for Jesus. Through knowing Jesus and bringing my hurts to Him, He has over time (and continues to) heal my heart and make me whole. Sometimes in ways so subtle I couldn't recall, other times, in the most abrupt surgery like moments that cut to my core and still other times, are moments of profound beauty that I will treasure always.

Jesus resumed talking to the people, but now tenderly. "The Father has given me all these things to do and say. This is a unique Father-Son operation, coming out of Father and Son intimacies and knowledge. No one knows the Son the way the Father does, nor the Father the way the Son does. But I'm not keeping it to myself; I'm ready to go over it line by line with anyone willing to listen.

"Are you tired? Worn out? Burned out on religion? Come to me. Get away with me and you'll recover your life. I'll show you how to take a real rest. Walk with me and work with me—watch how I do it. Learn the unforced rhythms of grace. I won't lay anything heavy or ill-fitting on you. Keep company with me and you'll learn to live freely and lightly."
Matthew 11:27-30 MSG

Take the journey, freedom is waiting.

So, friends, there is no shelf. It doesn't exist.

How can something like this exist when there is no consistent rationale for it? Every person has decided for themselves what 'the shelf' looks like, yet people with the same struggles or reasons are happily single, dating, engaged or even married.

Sometimes the shelf enables justification to ignore the flicker of hope that may lie within.
Sometimes the shelf is again another reason to explain to yourself why you are single.
Sometimes it is a line in the sand that protects your heart from further rejection.
Sometimes it is easier to reject ourselves before someone else has the opportunity to.

I admit, some people will stay single all their days, but that does not confirm the existence of the shelf. The shelf indicates a lack of something in the individual; a lack of worth, lack of youthfulness or beauty. In every case, it decreases the perception of your value and distances you from relational involvement. The shelf is based upon what you are not, it does not place value and celebrate who you are.

So, if you find this resonating with you; sitting on a 'shelf' of your creation, limiting the abundance of life that God has for you. Climb on down, dust yourself off and let's get to living!

Being in a relationship is one of the ways we interact with the world around us, it is not a status of worth.

Masquerade Ball

I walked into church one day desperately looking around for someone, *anyone*, I knew so I didn't look and feel so alone. My eyes landed on some familiar faces. I walked over and joined the conversation, trying to hide my awkwardness at feeling alone. I gently stood nearby, hoping I would feel like I fit, with a longing to make *actual* friends.

I casually listened to the conversation.

Soon there was a lull and the social leader, an extrovert, who I found insincere at the time, turned to me and said, "how are you Bethany?" Wanting to roll my eyes in annoyance, I thought 'as if you really care'. I did, however, rally my faculties to politely respond, "good thank you, how are you?"

The conversation continued on in a casual tone until the service started. I awkwardly took a seat, feeling so disconnected. I did not feel like I belonged, but, all my striving had successfully accomplished one thing; I had passed the test. I had politely replied, and my mask, for this beautiful masquerade ball, was still perfectly in-tact.

This is how many of us live our lives. We project a façade, without ever really letting anyone see or know the real us. At the heart of this mask is a deep seeded insecurity.

I struggled with insecurity for many years. For a long time, I presented who I thought everyone wanted to see, wearing the mask that fit the occasion or people in attendance. It was only away from the crowd that I was truly myself. How sad that I felt I had to conform to fit in? How sad that many people never got to know who I really was?

So, what do we do with insecurities?

Well, there are many great practical things you can do, but for me, there is one thing that helped dispel insecurity.

The cliché answer would be to say, 'trust God'. When you're in each of these situations, all you need to do is trust God. Yet, how can you trust Him if you aren't certain of His heart towards you?

This *really* hit home for me several years ago.

I was in a season of great pain, having done everything right and yet, still struggling to hold onto God. Whilst on holidays, driving toward a lookout in Tasmania, a podcast by Wayne Jacobsen pierced my soul; **"you cannot trust God until you know how much you are loved!"**

It hit me. *I did not know how much the Father loved me.*

I wish I could say my insecurities dissipated that day, but no! What did begin to dissipate was the false image I had held of myself. My heart was a mix of excitement in the revelation and realisation that this acknowledgement was my reality. Truth had dawned a new day, that led to a deep and real heart journey.

Insecurities stem from fear, and fear cannot be resolved simply by trust. Fear must be resolved by the realisation that one is loved; *that one is safe and secure in love.*

There is no room in love for fear. Well-formed love banishes fear. Since fear is crippling, a fearful life — fear of death, fear of judgment — is one not yet fully formed in love.
1 John 4:18 MSG

The key to overcoming insecurity is being loved by God. Embark on the journey, because truly, there is nothing better!

*He was looked down on and passed over,
a man who suffered, who knew pain firsthand.
One look at him and people turned away.
We looked down on him, thought he was scum.
But the fact is, it was our pains he carried—
our disfigurements, all the things wrong with us.
We thought he brought it on himself,
that God was punishing him for his own failures.
But it was our sins that did that to him,
that ripped and tore and crushed him—our sins!
He took the punishment, and* **that made us whole**.
Through his bruises we get healed.
Isaiah 53:3-5 MSG

*Pour out all your worries and stress upon him and leave
them there, for he always tenderly cares for you.*
1 Peter 5:7 TPT

Celebrate

There are many statements we hear that can be weighted with expectation.

"Your clock is ticking."
"You're getting on in age."
"It is better to be a young parent."
"There won't be any good partners left."
"If you don't get married soon, you'll miss one."
"It'll happen at the right time."
"It'll happen when you're ready."
"I got married around your age."
"I always thought you'd get married later in life."
"The longer you stay single, the harder it will be to adjust when you get married."

When it comes to people's words, there are thousands of comments that can create pressure and expectation. Sometimes as single people we can defensively respond with comments about our life as a single; the joys of no kids, sleeping in, financial independence and so on. Yet truthfully, we wish for more… and perhaps even secretly we are hurt that our desires are a little carelessly overlooked. Inwardly, we are crying out at times, 'do you think I wanted it this way?'

Recently over lunch, two women asked after me to one of my good friends. They went on to ask if I was still single; receiving an affirmative answer, one woman responded, "God has her on her own journey, getting her ready!"

When the story was relayed to me, *truthfully,* I was livid. As was my friend.

"Ready for what? Do these women, because they're married, think their character and personalities trump those who are not yet married. Do they realise that statement reflects upon their limited understanding of singleness?"

Together, we scoffed and ranted at such small-minded people.

Sometime later, I was called on my attitude and Holy Spirit showed me, though their attitude or understanding around singleness may not have been correct, neither was mine. I promptly repented and steered my heart in a new direction.

People's comments communicate expectations, understanding and attitudes that can greatly affect our hearts. Like a sharp pain to our heart, these comments can reveal in us our own disappointments, rejection, inabilities or even our lack of love for others and validation of their point of view.

Take it to God.

> *If we boast that we have no sin, we're only fooling ourselves and are strangers to the truth. But if we freely admit our sins when his light uncovers them, he will be faithful to forgive us every time. God is just to forgive us our sins because of Christ, and he will continue to cleanse us from all unrighteousness.*
> *1 John 1:8-9 TPT*

Let the sin of offence go; choose to forgive people who have disappointed, pressured or rejected you. Invite God to speak into your story, emotions and desires afresh.

Instead of looking at what should or could be, shift your focus to **celebrate what is**.

What is.

What are the beauties and benefits of your current season? What do you love about being single? What do you choose to see?

Being single, for me, is a great joy! (Okay, most of the time it is a great joy!!) Sure, I've had, even still have, times when I deeply struggle, cry my eyes out, question God, go to the Word for a word, hope to all hope that this time it won't end fruitlessly. However, at the end of the day, I choose to value what I have and follow God's leading.

What do you choose?

Let me tell you a story…

A few years ago, I resigned from my full-time job in response to the Holy Spirit leading, to study full-time again. However, the decision to study was only secondary to the location Holy Spirit was calling me to. Of all the places in the world, I was being called *back home*.

I'd been out of home for nearly a decade, and never in a million years had I imagined God asking me to move from the city of Adelaide back to the small *(very small)* town I came from. God was calling me back to live, yep you guessed it, with my parents.

Just prior to my departure from Adelaide, I had lunch with one of my colleagues. Whilst conversing over sushi, they enthusiastically said: "Beth, this is your year!" Vibrantly indicating that I was going to meet a strapping man that year *(most likely wearing moleskins and RM Williams, if people's assumptions about what all country people look like are to be believed)*.

However, I knew that wasn't so. As kindly as I could I rebuffed the statement and acknowledged one of the key reasons God was calling me back home.

You see, God wasn't just calling me back home just to study, or to have more time to travel, to lower my expenses, or to be close to family. I knew one of the main reasons God was calling me home was to *restore my relationship with my Dad*.

I also knew that God's story for my love life was secondary to this.

I live in response to Jesus, out of intimacy with Him, and I have learnt (and continue to learn) that I can trust His leading. This isn't a figuratively, nice sounding cliché; this is my reality. My relationship with Jesus brings clarity and understanding to every part of my life, what I like to call *my every day*. The more I know God and live in intimacy with Him, the more I rest and flourish in my season.

Christ's leading gives context to our circumstance, and even when we don't understand, we can honestly be okay with not knowing, because we know deeply the one who knows.

If we believe that God has our best, what then is our response to our life and current circumstances, including being single?

Driven By The External

While having brunch with some friends one of them started sharing about their current season. I felt like I was looking in a mirror, as my friend explained how she perceives that her life must appear to be moving forward in an attempt to justify her singleness.

What appearance do we feel compelled to give? What factors influence our decision making? And why do we feel that our singleness needs to be justified?

The world pulls, promotes and pushes us to want more, to do more, and to be more. Mounted pressure from abrupt campaigns to office banter can provoke us to question ourselves, fuelling decisions to gain further acceptance.

These judgements, perceived and real, place pressure to make our lives 'look' like they are moving forward. The deep need for acceptance and the fear of people drive many of us to think according to other people's perceptions rather than who we are.

There is a drive for the external.

For some it is buying a home, a newer car, having the right friends, having a nightlife that looks impressive, travelling to far off places, being highly involved in church, getting promoted at work. Not negative in themselves, but, if they become a crutch to make singleness more acceptable, they are unhealthy.

I recommend you take a moment to confess all areas where things, places, or people have become a crutch. Repent and thank God for His forgiveness. Know, when Christ sets you free, you are free indeed.

It is as though there is a silent assumption that external things matter more than who we are. That the life we live on the outside is worth more than the person we are on the inside. Few celebrate the goodness of who people are, whilst many celebrate the things they have accomplished.

I encourage you to choose to forgive all people from whom you have felt judged. Speak out forgiveness and ask God to fill you afresh with His Holy Spirit.

God has our best at heart, striving and living with the judgements and pressure of others does not reinforce this, *it destroys it!* We begin to question God's heart for us, question whether God has forgotten us. We make assumptions and jump to conclusions, creating an incorrect worldview that leads to internal conflict and unhealthy decisions.

If you have allowed the judgments or pressure from others to affect your relationship with God, confess this to Him and thank Him for His forgiveness.

Following Jesus has never been about placing weight on the external over the internal.

Expectations

Once, when working as a ministry assistant, the Chief Financial Officer came into my office and said *"Bethany, you would be great in the army. You do what you're told and expect everyone else to also"*. I laughed, fully aware of how much truth was in that statement.

Expectations project performance standards for people to reach. In situations *such as* work and sport the bar set assists in producing high standards and results. In relationships, however, expectations can be damaging.

In relationships, many of us take on the perceived expectations of others and develop unrealistic expectations for ourselves. Our lives become trapped, as we shape ourselves to become someone else's idea of who we *should* be.

I tried my hardest to live up to the expectations of others, I also placed high expectations on myself. In an attempt to be successful and gain acceptance, I lived a life striving to do everything I *should* do, to become the version of myself that everyone saw I *could* be. I gave everything I had, but, it was never enough. Sadly, it didn't stop there. I not only lived under this pressure, but, I readily placed it on others.

Expectations in relationships cause us not only to believe something will happen, but, that it *should*. This places pressure on the other person to perform in accordance with *our* thinking. Instead of giving people room to show us who they are, expectations set a standard on who we think they *should be*.

Constant pressure to fall in line with what we see, or desire, misses the entire point of relationships; *to know the other person*. How can we truly know the other person, when our view is coloured with what we think they should be, or should do? Our relationships become focused on performance (or the lack of!), robbing the other person, the opportunity to reveal, and be accepted, for who they really are.

This leads to a performance centred dynamic that promotes conformity and disempowers freedom of choice. **Ouch!**

Singleness can be a magnet for expectations, from family, friends and society. We easily get caught in the trap to meet the expectations of those around us. We take on the subtleties in conversation, compare our lives to others, succumb to negative emotions and strive on. Within time, our identity becomes wrapped up in the fact that we are *still* single.

It's like navigating a mind-field!

Our lives become an obstacle course set by the expectations of ourselves and others.

Maybe you're like this?

Do you live in a pressure cooker full of expectations? Do you allow those expectations to affect you? Is your life defined by what you or others think your life "should" look like?

Surely there is another way?

Christ did not set you free from the world for you to become enslaved to the expectations of yourself or others.

Christ came to set you free; to no longer conform to the ideal of others, or to your own shifting standards. To know you are wholly and unconditionally accepted, and loved, under grace. No longer trapped, controlled or coerced, but free, truly free.

Expectations can breed captivity. It is only by believing these expectations that we give them the power to hold us captive. You have a choice; to walk in expectation or in freedom.

Whether single, dating, engaged, or married, let's pursue freedom in Christ and from there develop healthy relationships with one another; through healthy communication and shared vision, not expectation to conform to one person's ideals.

Christ has set us free to live a free life.
So take your stand! Never again let anyone
put a harness of slavery on you.
Galatians 5:1 MSG

For me, being single has been far richer being free than it ever was being a slave.

+ + + + +

As single people, many of us have specific expectations on God, on *what age we will get married, on what the person will be like,* and *how God will bring it about.* This can lead to disappointment, or control to make something happen, and both can lead to unhealthy decisions. Unless God has directly spoken to you, I encourage you to communicate your desires, but, let go of holding God accountable to *your* expectations and standards. Know God and rest your hope in who He is.

A Heroine

Singleness is a constant balance, sometimes even a conflict, between hope and contentment. I don't believe there is a recipe for this balance as it is an individual journey, but, I do believe God is greatly interested in your contentment and your hopes. Learning to live contentedly, whilst holding hope is a tension, not only in singleness, but, in many areas of life.

It can be found. There is a place where hope and contentment are lived out in unity.

I recently made a new friend. She is a former Overseas Missionary Fellowship (OMF) missionary, who primarily ministered to the Mien people group, of Northern Thailand, for over 50 years *and* never married.

We sat in her lounge room conversing about life. The conversation turned to singleness. We reflected that life is full of the unexpected, both joys and heartbreaks. I commented that the only guarantees in life are that God loves me and God is good.

She knowingly added... *and that you can trust Him.*

> *"It is only in knowing that we are loved*
> *that we can truly trust God."*
> Wayne Jacobsen, He Loves Me

But you are God's chosen treasure—priests who are kings, a spiritual "nation" set apart as God's devoted ones. He called you out of darkness to experience his marvellous light, and now he claims you as his very own. He did this so that you would broadcast his glorious wonders throughout the world. For at one time you were not God's people, but now you are. At one time you knew nothing of God's mercy, because you hadn't received it yet, but now you are drenched with it!
1 Peter 2:9-10 TPT

in the real world

Some Days

Being single is not always easy. It can be tremendously hard. Some days it can be almost unbearable.

The deep longing and desire to share your life with someone. For someone to *know* you and still *love* you, for someone to plan holidays with, for someone to dream a life with or simply to know that no matter what life throws your way that you are not alone. These are weighty desires!

We can appreciate friendship, and the many other fulfilling ways that we share our lives with others. However, it's important to be honest about the pain and emptiness that can be felt. Being single is not all sleep-ins, travel and fun. It is normal day to day life lived, sometimes feeling *very alone*.

If you feel this way, it is okay.

There is no quick fix when it comes to matters of the heart. Capturing every thought, and appreciating what we currently have, can certainly help keep our heart healthy, but, I do not want to ignore, that sometimes it is not easy being single.

It is unexplainable at times.
The ache inside is real and often raw, and it should not be despised or ignored.

God created humans as relational beings and at times the emotions of being human reach a crescendo of emptiness. Though we cannot live here, it does not mean it should not be felt, acknowledged and shared.

Sometimes, it is okay to not be okay.

> *"So now, all alone or not, you gotta walk ahead.*
> *Thing to remember is if we're all alone,*
> *then we're all together in that too."*
> *- Cecelia Ahern, P.S. I Love You*

I was washing up. Mark had the tedious job of wiping up. Conversation was light and fun as many others swirled around the kitchen. Our dialogue happened to turn to relationships and Mark asked how many relationships I had been in. After I commented, Mark leaned back against the bench, tea-towel and dish paused in hand. He looked down, as though deeply moved, and said: "that must be really hard".

It can be.

I have hopes that will last for years whether I meet someone or not, but some days, that doesn't matter. *Some days it just plain hurts.*

Sometimes it can be hard to explain these feelings to our friends. Hard to think logically and make sense of our thoughts. We struggle to understand *'what the heck is going on!'* So, go ahead, get your favourite trackies on, curl up on your couch, watch your favourite film and have another piece of chocolate.

It's okay to have a day here and there where you're asking God hard questions, feeling a little low, or going through something that compounds the fact that 'yep, you're still single'. However, if your 'some days' become your every day we have a problem. Here are some thoughts for you...

Your singleness does not define you, your mood does not define you. God defines you and He is the source of truth and value.

Acknowledge how you feel, but do not allow your feelings to define the course of your life. It is okay to be single and it is okay if it hurts at times, give yourself permission to feel. However, don't live there! Emotions come and go; they were not designed to stay.

Whatever your preferred method of communication or expression is, make sure you are purposeful about connecting with others during this time. Talk it out, walk it out, sing it out if you have to. Do not hold and dwell on it, this will only lead to self-pity and destruction.

Lastly, if your couch is becoming your best friend, actively seek to find a new one. Join a tennis club, volunteer at the local community centre, meet your neighbours, plan a holiday with friends. Live life and love the life you live.

> *"Friendship is unnecessary, like philosophy, like art...*
> *It has no survival value; rather it is one of those*
> *things that give value to survival."*
> C.S. Lewis

Some days can be hard, allow them to be felt, but recondition your mind and spirit to relish the beauty of your everyday.

A thief has only one thing in mind—he wants to steal, slaughter, and destroy. But I have come to give you everything in abundance, more than you expect— life in its fullness until you overflow!
John 10:10 TPT

Jesus was single.

Ponder that.

Intimacy

For a university project, I conducted a survey around singleness. In one question, each person was asked to list things they liked and disliked about being single. The respondents could select from a range of statements that summarised their reflections. Out of the twelve options, the following were the most prevalent responses; *having someone to adventure with, having someone to talk to* and *I want to be loved*.

Maybe these resonate with you, also. I know they have with me at various times. Though they resonate, it does not mean that they should be the prevailing struggles in our lives. Singleness, dating, engagement and marriage each have their own struggles, but, I do not believe that these challenges should ever triumph in defining our season or indeed our life.

Recently, I was sitting in a university hall in Toronto, listening to a man share his story to a few hundred young adults as to why he had chosen celibacy. During his talk, he made a profound observation; *"in our culture, we have pretty much collapsed intimacy and sex into each other"*. He went on to say, *"you can have a lot of sex and not be having any intimacy. You can have a lot of intimacy without having sex."* Our world teaches us that to be truly loved we must be in a sexual relationship. People become activists of this misguided belief; even in the schoolyard when peer pressure begins, we begin to take on the lie that intimacy is found in sex.

Does this mean Jesus never experienced intimacy on earth? Or this man that has chosen celibacy? What about you and I? Can we not experience intimacy as singles? The truth is that you can have sex without intimacy, and intimacy without sex. This is not to reduce sex or negate the power of marriage, but to reveal the truth that intimacy can be experienced by all.

Intimacy is vulnerability in safety that produces closeness; emotionally, spiritually and or physically. Intimacy can be experienced as a single person. I encourage you to build friendships that provide you with people to adventure with, someone to talk to and make you feel loved. This is living!

Fear and Desire

Fear

As we drove through the suburbs of Sydney, I shared my story with a friend, giving reasons why God's intention may be for me to remain single. Hailey disagreed, rebuking my own conclusion and confidently affirming that I would, one day, get married.

But how did she know? Really know? Fear began to settle in around my heart.

As Fear gripped my heart that day, I became acutely aware that I didn't trust God in this area. I didn't want to remain single forever and feared that God's best would not be *what I wanted*.

'What I wanted'.

Oh God, how many times do we as humans ask You to bless *our* plans? If it is God's best, why would I not want it?

It is fear that holds many of us captive.

Fear ... *what if I never get married; what if I say yes to a date, I don't even know if I like him; what if she doesn't say yes; what if I am still single in five years?*

Fear so easily becomes the driving force in our emotions and decisions; fear can cause us to retreat, to dive in too quickly or to remain stuck in the mud. Fear repels God and like a magnet, draws us further into its grip.

Desire

I was baking (a somewhat irregular occurrence) and Lissette turned to focus on me. She animatedly described a young man she knew; the loving nanna-like affection she felt for him was obvious. It was like she was talking directly to me. Everything Lisette said sounded like it was a 'male order' just for me - my desire ran like wildfire.

Has your heart ever run wildly? Have you ever fantasied about someone for days or months on end? Have you ever said 'yes' forgetting all logic, even godliness?

God created each of us with a desire for relationship, with a sexual drive and, also, gave us individual desires for our own lives. However, these can easily get blended with unhealthy desires we have nurtured, distorted or fantasized. We end up feeding the misconstrued desires rather than Godly hope. We make rash and selfish decisions, though they feel good, they may not be in alignment with God's desires.

Desire is much like fire, it is beautiful and mesmerising, but if unguarded can cause great destruction and loss.

Being single can be difficult when it comes to sexual and emotional desire, but it does not mean it should be indulged in. Stand firm and guard against distortion.

+ + + + +

Fear and desire are the two areas that have attempted to pull me from alignment with Christ. In many heart to heart conversations, I have observed that they are also common challenges for other singles. Though fear and desire might feel good or be a method for self-protection, neither is freedom. Living in Christ is true freedom, but freedom is not gained through lack of effort, one must be vigilant.

> *God, I invite your searching gaze into my heart.*
> *Examine me through and through;*
> *find out everything that may be hidden within me.*
> *Put me to the test and sift through all my anxious cares.*
> *See if there is any path of pain I'm walking on,*
> *and lead me back to your glorious, everlasting ways —*
> *the path that brings me back to you.*
> *Psalm 139:23-24 TPT*

I encourage you to be humble and courageous in your walk with Christ. Acknowledge weakness and struggle and be courageous enough to deal with it. Our single season is not to be lived out independent from following Jesus, it is to be submitted under His Lordship.

*For His divine power has bestowed
on us [absolutely] everything necessary for
[a dynamic spiritual] life and godliness, through true
and personal knowledge of Him who called us
by His own glory and excellence.
2 Peter 1:3 AMP*

Puzzles

A puzzle is a picture that slowly unfolds as each piece is added.

When it comes to matters of the heart, we are brilliant puzzle builders!

Before he's even looked your way, he's ticked every eagerly anticipated box. Before she's even said anything intelligent, she's caught your eye. He said something nice to you in passing. She smiled when she said, 'hello'. He gives eye contact in conversation. She can sing. He likes to cook. She works out.

We have analysed *every single detail* of the interaction, convinced that this piece fits right into the puzzle. We are excellent at writing stories and building lives, the problem is; many of them are in our imagination.

When we were younger my siblings and I would play cowboys and Indians or schools, these were our favourite imaginary games. As we grow up, we don't lose this, we internalise it. And most of the time it revolves around grand adventures of travel, careers and love, *especially love*.

Yet, often our puzzles are left unfinished on the table.

All that remains are fragments of a dream once held, accompanied with the feelings of failure and disappointment.

How do we stop our heart running wild? How do we take risks whilst guarding our heart?

Disappointment is the result of unmet expectations.

Have you ever dreamt of a life only to have it come crashing down? Have you imagined a relationship that really wasn't what you thought? What about right now, where is the attention of your heart?

Our expectations might seem reasonable enough - we tell ourselves we want to make a new friend, maybe get one more text or maybe, just maybe, get asked for coffee to get to know someone. Yet really at the heart of it we are hoping for more; marriage, intimacy, family, adventure, the building of a life together. Our expectations are so high in this puzzle we are building, that when unmet or delay comes, it's a *long* way back to reality and the disappointment is all consuming.

Does this mean we never dare to hope? Or, try not to *really want* another text message? Never. I love stories of potential love and new love and I have hope that I will marry and have gorgeous children one day. This hope, however, rests in God, not in every man I like. When this weight of expectation shifts to the man I like, I set him up to produce life for me. God is my master, not any man.

Let me add, this does not mean you don't say 'yes' to having coffee, you don't ask her on a picnic, that you don't send that message. It means that you hold it loosely, while you rest your hope in God.

Expression

Freedom of expression can mean a multitude of things and conjures up various ideas in each of our minds. Expression involves every part of us; our minds, will, emotions, body and spirit. We are not one-dimensional, physical people, we express our identities through our diverse range of capacities to communicate. We should not single out our physicality as the sole vehicle for sexual expression which God designed and intended to be holistic.

Now, it would be "easy", if I had five steps to healthy sexual expression, but I do not. Nor, do I really wish to attempt to list them, as I dislike tick-boxes and steps that claim to offer the perfect solution. I believe in God's principles outlined in the Word, centred on a relationship with Him that helps fashion our hearts and lives.

The key to living healthy expression is not found in do's and don'ts but in knowing God, His Word and acknowledging that His thoughts on all topics matter more than anyone else's.

+ + + + +

Knowing how important it is to dive into this area of our lives, I want to ask you some questions. Not, so I can give what I have discovered, but, to stir you to seek out God's thoughts for yourself.

- How do you currently express your sexuality? Is it a healthy expression, or does it take advantage of another person?
- Are you emotionally involved with someone of the opposite sex? Does the relationship provide healthy expression, or does it create dependency and mask insecurity?
- Are you over-promising and under-delivering in your flirtatious encounters?
- Do you feel guilty after any sort of emotional, or physical expression of sexuality? What do you do with that guilt? How do you think God perceives you as a result?
- Who are you closest to? How do you relate to them?
- What does the Bible say about: lust, self-control and covenant relationships?
- On the days when you're really struggling with being single and having pent up sexual desire, what normally happens?
- Do you masturbate? What do you think God thinks of masturbation?
- Do you ask the Holy Spirit to help you with self-control when needed? To develop patience and strength of spirit that endures?
- Does your love for others govern your treatment of them, or your own agenda and sexual desires?
- What does healthy sexual expression look like?

These are weighty questions, I know.

I am raising them as an avenue to reflect honestly upon, and perhaps open conversations for you to have, with God and your church community. As singles, so much of this is *not talked about*, but what good does that do? How does that help us live the single life well?

Just because conversations are hard, it doesn't mean we avoid them. Healthy expression is for many a great struggle in being single. Therefore, we must be honest with our God community; ourselves, those who disciple us, and those we disciple, but most importantly, God Himself, valuing His opinions and thoughts above all.

It is in relationship with God that change occurs. Religion and self-help ideology has taught us that character development is dependent upon *our* willpower to avoid or reject evil and its temptations. However, Galatians teaches us a profound truth.

> *The fruit **produced by the Holy Spirit** within you is divine love in all its various expressions. This love is revealed through: joy that overflows, peace that subdues, patience that endures, kindness in action, a life full of virtue, faith that prevails, gentleness of heart, and strength of spirit.*
> Galatians 5:22-23TPT

A profound aspect of seeing the fruits of the spirit is that *the Holy Spirit produces these in us.* The Holy Spirit *produces* fruit, not us. As you reflect upon your expression as a single person, I implore you to desire right living and at the same time, take the pressure off to achieve change through self-effort. In all areas of life, including sexuality, embrace Holy Spirit as the change agent.

If Holy Spirit is the change agent, what is our role?

> *"As you yield freely and fully to the dynamic life and power of the Holy Spirit, you will abandon the cravings of your self-life."*
> Galatians 5:16 TPT

Our role is to yield to the Spirit and involve Him in every part of our world: work, finance, dreams, friendships, family and sexuality. As we yield, He changes us and the fruit of the spirit is the evidence of His influence.

Forget religion, embrace relationship with the Spirit!

+ + + + +

Here are some points to ponder as you seek God and establish a deeper understanding of healthy expression in your season;

- God is the real deal, not a man in the clouds. God created our sexual desires, knows our past, present and future. Jesus was single and understands life as a single man, well past the "marriageable" age.
- God wants a relationship with you. He isn't into religion, doesn't place condemnation on you and loves you more than you can imagine.
- Secrets grow and fester in darkness. Secrets lose some of their power when brought into the light, therefore, talk out your struggles with trusted people, seek prayer and Godly solutions.
- Some of us may not have quality families to do life with. For those who do, family can be a form of positive expression as we live in a community of giving and receiving love, even if by distance.
- Make it your mission to become a master of friendship, be the best friend that you can be.

God is interested in the reality of our everyday lives: *our struggles, heartaches, hurts, joys, dreams.* **Jesus didn't come to save us for Sunday services,** ***He came to redeem our everyday.***

The greatest relationship we will ever have is our relationship with God.

Unknown

Have you ever thought about the fact that your season of singleness could come to an end at any moment?

I am currently sitting in a café writing whilst looking out over the ocean. It is a beautiful sight as people are mingling around me, and living active lives outside the window that frames my view. There is the possibility that I could catch someone's eye, so much so that they could muster the courage to ask to join me. Depending on the conversation and connection, my single season could be transitioning.

There is a potential the next person to join your team at work could be your future partner. There is potential a new woman will move to town, make your church home and as they say, 'the rest is history'. There is potential you will strike up a conversation with the person sitting next to you, on your next flight, resulting in many more conversations. There is potential you will receive a Facebook message from a person who has finally found the courage to tell you they'd like to get to know you more.

There is potential for your single season to end at any moment.

I have a friend who met her husband whilst visiting a girlfriend at her home.
My mum moved from the country to the city, where she met my Dad.
Samuel and Amanda met whilst at a Bible College in a class of ten.
My best friend moved from South Africa to Western Australia where she met her husband.
Samson was on holidays on the coast, he walked into a café where Ellie was working.
My brother accepted one of the university offers he received, where he met his now fiancé.

I find this one of the harder aspects of singleness, constantly holding out hope whilst remaining content. Being content in the mystery, in the unknown.

The tension of hope and contentment is not isolated to singleness; it is entwined in most of our seasons.

Friends of mine have been trying for a baby for a few years.
Another friend has been enduring a long season of difficulty at work.
Another has been sick for several years with many relapses in health.

In all seasons of the unknown, we have a choice to either be a victim in the tension, or enter into a deeper dependency upon God.

Thankfully

Life often reminds me that God's thoughts are higher than mine.
Promising to go beyond my limited understanding.

*"For my thoughts are not your thoughts, neither are
your ways my ways," declares the Lord.
"As the heavens are higher than the earth,
so are my ways higher than your ways
and my thoughts than your thoughts."
Isaiah 55:8-9*

*Who could ever wrap their minds around the riches of
God, the depth of his wisdom, and the marvel of his
perfect knowledge? Who could ever explain the wonder
of his decisions or search out the mysterious
way he carries out his plans?
Romans 11:33 TPT*

Thankfully we don't understand all of God's ways, for if we did
His omnipotence and majesty would be stripped away.

Whimsical Staircase

You know when you like someone, you can become infatuated with imagining their perfection and dream up that perfect life together.

STOP!

Now, let's talk reality.

When you like someone, they are not perfect, you are not perfect *(I know you're shocked!)*, and your life together will not be perfect.

When you marry someone, you don't marry their 'Sunday self', you don't marry the 'party version of them', you marry *their reality*.

> Love joyfully celebrates honesty ["reality" or "truth"]
> and finds no delight in what is wrong.
> 1 Corinthians 13:6 TPT

They work sixty hours a week, they don't read their bible every day, they can't sing, yet sing all the time, they hate doing housework, can't cook, their shirt is never tucked in, their feet smell, she doesn't feel relaxed without make-up on, she won't try new things, he doesn't enjoy the ambience of a restaurant, he doesn't know what cufflinks are, let alone own them, she chews gum loudly, he wears tracksuit pants out, his hands are always dirty from work, he doesn't like sleeping in on holidays, she likes too much chocolate, she likes expensive presents, he likes video-games... whatever. Reality.

As much as I love whimsical romance, we must be careful not to live in fantasy.

In a world of fantasy, one only considers the things they like, or areas they think will change, ignoring the little things and excluding reality. Hearts become wildly enchanted, in a world that is *not real*.

If you find yourself there, I encourage you to wind your way back down from that whimsical staircase, take off the grandeur and now think, do I still like this person?

Over the years, people have made the comment to me, "you're going to find the best man". As much as I love that this comment reflects their admiration of me as a person, it always leads me back to, that no matter who that (ever so lucky) person will be, that 'best man' will not be marrying the perceived reality of me, but *my reality*.

The person I marry marries my reality. The best things about me and the not so good. This reflection helps me walk back down the whimsical staircase to where I want to work on being the best version of myself.

I encourage you not to waste your precious single years on getting *carried away* with fantasy. We'll like people as singles (some of which will be great options!), but don't get *distracted* on living a life chasing a *perceived reality* of someone.

Forget fantasy, instead, let's become the people we want to be and build the reality we *want* to live in. Yes!

You're beautiful from head to toe, my dear love, beautiful beyond compare, absolutely flawless.
Song of Songs 4:7 MSG

Brick Castles

> *Be free from pride-filled opinions, for they will only harm your cherished unity. Don't allow self-promotion to hide in your hearts, but in authentic humility put others first and view others as more important than yourselves. Abandon every display of selfishness. Possess a greater concern for what matters to others instead of your own interests. And consider the example that Jesus, the Anointed One, has set before us. Let his mindset become your motivation.*
> Philippians 2:3-5 TPT

Bricks are made by compressing materials through a furnace so that all the elements fuse together. They are strong and durable. Bricks are made, stored in piles and then transported to be used to build a variety of things, including castles.

Imagine that every emotion to be expressed, thought worth sharing, daily routines and adventures are all bricks being produced in our lives. As they are created, they are placed in the brickyard. And we have the opportunity to ship them wherever we like in the world.

Every emotion, thought, and experience we have does not need to be shared. However, it can be! Our lives have the potential to build relationships *if shared*.

When you share aspects of your life with others, it is like setting a brick in place, on the masterpiece, of the relationship you're building. Every time you have an emotion to be expressed, thought worth sharing, adventure awaiting… it can be a brick left lying in the brickyard, or can be a brick to a castle.

What friendships are you building? How are you investing into those relationships? Or do you tend to avoid initiating connection? Do you live largely in isolation? Are you leaving bricks piled up that could be used to build something? If so, how can you be more intentional?

I do not want to get to the end of my life and think; *I could have built a castle but instead, I have a pile of bricks. I could have built a relationship, but instead, I kept it all to myself.*

I am a very open and transparent person, but, also private (*a dichotomy I know*!), sometimes, finding it hard to be vulnerable in the middle of something. The other day I was spending time with someone, who I really want to build a deeper friendship with, and I intentionally chose to be vulnerable. Why? Because I want my relationship with her to be a castle, not a regrettable pile of bricks.

We have the power to build our relationships, married or single! As singles, we don't always have "a person" that gets our first tears after an exhausting day, the peak of excitement after good news, that one person to experience an adventure with… we have *many* people to whom we can invest in, build with and be intentional.

"Here's to the ones who dream
Foreign as they may seem.
Here's to the hearts that ache
Here's to the mess we make."
Mia, La La Land

Dream

> *So why would I fear the future? For your goodness and love pursue me all the days of my life.*
> Psalm 23:6a TPT

Many people have dreams of marrying one day. Some have their dream dress or attire selected. Others, the music and dance moves! Still others, dream of honeymoon locations. I have personally had more conversations with women about these marital aspirations than men. I have known women to buy wedding magazines just for fun and why not? They are beautifully inspiring, and creative. However, there are some that dream beyond the white dress allowing their heart to become consumed with the pursuit of marriage. This pursuit becomes their supreme dream on which happiness rests.

Aleisha was raised in a Christian family. She had a strong personal relationship with God. She had done 'everything' right in regard to upholding Christian principles. Aleisha really wanted to meet the right person and if meeting someone correlated with brownie points for faithfulness, she would have scored high!

But guess what? It doesn't.

Aleisha remained single for over a decade after we first met; whether single, dating or married, there is life to be experienced and loved.

You can dream about getting married, but if this is your central dream and your life is hinging on this becoming a reality, something needs to change. Allow other dreams to come to the forefront.

You are not waiting for your life to start, life has already started! It is there for the taking!

For some, I realise this dream is not fuelled by culture, or expectation, but, is simply your deepest and sincerest desire. I acknowledge that this dream is good and I am sorry that one of your deepest desires is not yet realised. But, I also encourage you to dream.

Don't fear to dream new dreams.

Don't shy away from embracing singleness or reaching a point of contentment. Learn to embrace new dreams that cause a flourishing in your world. And always, always continue to develop and invest in your relationship with God.

Singleness is a tremendous opportunity. It is an opportunity to accomplish dreams and life aspirations in a unique way.

Some of you may have dormant dreams that you have not allowed to expand and be realised. Revive them. Dust them off and be intentional to make them happen.

Some of you don't have many dreams at all. I encourage you to start dreaming. Create space in your life to think about the things *you* would love to do.

Don't look at the lives of others or attempt to fulfil their dreams, *dream your dreams*.

What makes you come alive? What makes you roar with laughter? What adventure have you always thought, *'imagine if...'*?

Your personal desires make you unique; *what are they?* Maybe to work overseas, buy or build a house, move town, go on a particular holiday, start a business, run a marathon, join a dance crew, play in a badminton team. The options are endless and are specific to your authentic identity.

Dreams keep us alive and young. Plus, I think there's nothing better than doing something you love or having something thrilling to look forward to.

You, in partnership with God, are the designer of your life. You can't wait for someone else to create it.

Learn to love the season you're in, and cherish the unique opportunities that lie within your reach.

I have been taught from a very young age that if you are happy single, you will be happy married. Happiness is not obtained in a person, it is the fruit of a healthy soul.

Do yourself a favour and dream.

Bye for now...

I hope these thoughts have been insightful *(and even entertaining at times!)* I pray that they have promoted change in you, brought you into greater freedom and moved you closer to Jesus.

It is my prayer that we will be generations who follow Jesus in obedience over comfort. To go on the journey knowing we're deeply loved by God and allow that to dramatically change our world. From that, submit to His Lordship and actively pursue holiness in all areas, including singleness.

In all the adventures yet to have, let's keep following Jesus.

Thanks for reading!

Bethany

Ken Cheal

Photographer

Ken Cheal is an amateur photographer specialising in candid and landscape photos. His eye for capturing everyday moments, nature and details are strengths in his photography. He's a builder by trade and after hours can often be found behind a lens, or with a guitar in hand.

Instagram @kenchill_27

Facebook ken.cheal

Thank You

Mum for reading, listening, editing, re-reading and more. Words never do who you are justice; you have helped shaped who I am and this work of art. Thank you for your constant love and sacrifice. **Dad**, for your love, constant patience and wisdom. Thanks for living by faith in who you are. *I love you both.* To **my family and friends**, who make my life a great and glorious adventure. **Jonathan** for your love and value of me and the way they call out further depth in who I am, and for your insightful critic that helped reshape this work. **Sophie** for loving me deeply, your heart is so treasured, you are a gift! I am so thankful this journey has been with you. **Emily** for your constant prayers and heart for this project, what a beautiful blessing you are! **Naomi**, I am incredibly thankful for you and our friendship. Thank you for your belief in me and in this content. **Annabel** for your encouragement and belief; seriously, this journey has been way more fun with you in it! **Rina** for being the friend a girl could only dream of. God moved you from Busselton just for me. **Cathy**, **Beth** and **Amber** thanks for being heart friends and praying this in with me.

Plus, special mention to those who have helped pull this project off... **Ken Cheal** for taking on the unexpected and capturing the beauty of everyday. To all those who were willing to be photographed, thank you for joining the adventure! **Kristy Mills** for your belief, gifts and generosity; you are exceptional. **Emma Hale** thanks for seeing my heart and investing into this project. You have been a miracle and blessing in this being completed.

Most of all, deepest thanks to **my favourite person;** for loving me unconditionally and for making me brave, you're my absolute favourite! This is because of you and for you.

www.ingramcontent.com/pod-product-compliance
Lightning Source LLC
Chambersburg PA
CBHW041927090426
42743CB00021B/3471